For Cynthia. And for Billy. For the joy of poetry. And for EW! —L.B.

To Alice. EW!! —Love, J.P.

Millbrook Press™
An imprint of Lerner Publishing Group, Inc.
241 First Avenue North
Minneapolis, MN 55401 USA

For reading levels and more information, look up this title at www.lernerbooks.com.

Additional design elements by: s_maria/Shutterstock; kokoshka/Shutterstock; TommyK/Alamy; Palomita/Shutterstock; jannoon028/Shutterstock.

Designed by Kimberly Morales.
Main body text set in Coventry ITC Std. Typeface provided by International Typeface Corporation.
The illustrations in this book were traditionally hand drawn with pencil and colored digitally.

Library of Congress Cataloging-in-Publication Data

Names: Brunelle, Lynn, author. | Patton, Julia, illustrator.
Title: Haiku ew! : celebrating the disgusting side of nature / Lynn Brunelle ; illustrated by Julia Patton.
Description: Minneapolis : Millbrook Press , 2024. | Audience: Ages 7–11 | Audience: Grades 2–3 | Summary: "These gross and engrossing haiku highlight thirteen animals (and a few fungi) and the exceptionally icky things they do! Accompanied by bonus facts that will delight—and disgust—readers of all ages" —Provided by publisher.
Identifiers: LCCN 2023021727 (print) | LCCN 2023021728 (ebook) | ISBN 9781728492506 (library binding) | ISBN 9798765619100 (epub)
Subjects: LCSH: Animals—Juvenile poetry. | Haiku, American. | Children's poetry, American. | Animals—Juvenile literature. | BISAC: JUVENILE NONFICTION / Poetry / Humorous | LCGFT: Haiku. | Humorous poetry.
Classification: LCC PS3602.R8464 H35 2024 (print) | LCC PS3602.R8464 (ebook) | DDC 811/.6—dc23/eng/20230608

LC record available at https://lccn.loc.gov/2023021727
LC ebook record available at https://lccn.loc.gov/2023021728

Manufactured in the United States of America
1-53357-51237-10/24/2023

HAIKU, EW!

Celebrating the Disgusting Side of Nature

nectar → bee barf

LYNN BRUNELLE

illustrated by JuLia PattoN

poop

EW!

Millbrook Press / Minneapolis

Nature has been inspiring poetry and art for as long as humans have been out there enjoying the view. And why not?

Nature is beautiful!

It's magnificent!

It's amazing!

And it's also SUPER GROSS!

BEE barf

Ew!

caution

Fully formed toadlets
Pop out of bumps on Mom's back,
Erupting like zits.

Hey, so do you know what's really gross? Surinam toad birth. The flat marine toad looks like a dead leaf covered with little spots and bumps. But these little bumps pack a punch. When the female mates with a male, he fertilizes her eggs and glues them to her back. In a few days, her skin grows over the eggs and the babies develop underneath the skin. When they're ready, they burst out of their little pimple-like mounds on Mom's back and pop out fully formed. Ah, motherhood!

EW!

Ahh, that's better!

Steamy flamingo,
Your technique for staying cool?
Just poop on your legs!

poop

poop

EW!

FLAMINGO

notes →

poop ↑

Do you ever get desperately hot? Be happy you can reach for a fan or grab a cold drink. To keep cool, these hot pink birds poop on their own legs and feet. It's a clever trick called urohidrosis. Eventually, the sludge dries, leaving behind smelly white powder that protects their legs and feet from sunburn. Something to try the next time you run out of sunblock?

← poop

↑ poop

Thunderous bubbles
Erupt from schools of herring.
Secret fart fish talk.

HERRING

fish
Fart

For herring, farting is not just hot air. It serves an important function. These tiny fish actively push air out of their rectums in different tones to communicate with one another. No one has deciphered the fart-talk language or the meaning of the toots, but scientists have discovered that herring sip air at the surface so they can "speak" to one another in the water. That's one way to talk in "school"!

EW!

Lush, sun-gold honey
Brewed from delicate nectar.
It's really bee barf.

When a honeybee lands on a flower, she slurps nectar and stores it in her "honey stomach"—a tiny pouch that scientists call her crop. Acids in her crop break down the nectar into sugar-building blocks.

When her crop is full, she heads back to the hive and spits the nectar into the mouth of a waiting bee. That bee passes it to the open mouth of another bee. This process is repeated over and over again, like a barfy game of telephone, until all the nectar is transformed into sugary honey and dribbled into a beeswax cell.

Ok, so if you want to get technical, honey isn't *true* barf, because the nectar is stored in the honey-stomach (crop). Bees have another "stomach," called a proventriculus, that they use for eating and digesting. The regurgitated nectar is upchucked from the crop, not the actual stomach. It's a fine line, but these details may be comforting.

Call it what you will, it goes down and comes back up over and over again, and the result is delicious drizzled on toast and dripped into tea!

barf

Bee's → knees

proventriculus

head   thorax   crop

abdomen

Glowworms in a cave

Sparkle like the midnight sky—

Luminous snot strands.

Glowworms are not actually worms at all. They are the baby larval stage of the flying gnat known as *Arachnocampa luminosa*, and they are always hunting. These babies cling to the ceilings of caves and "fish" for insects by spitting out thin strings of silk. The strands are dotted with glowing globules of sticky mucus, like a nasty string of beads.

Because the ceiling looks like a wide-open night sky, insects fly up and get tangled in the sparkly, sticky mucus blobs. The glowworm feels the tug and quickly sucks up the snotty thread like a strand of spaghetti, then gobbles up the insect. Talk about a spit take!

EW!

Frog wakes with the rain,
Covered with biting insects.
Sheds skin. Eats them all.

insects

The water-holding frog of Australia can live underground and go years without moving, eating, or drinking. This is helpful during dry spells. But when the rains come, the frog wakes up and digs out of the soil. Hungry insects immediately jump on it. But this frog has a gluey little secret. Its skin is sticky, so the insects that land on it get trapped. Eventually, the frog sheds its skin and swallows it—insects and all.

sheds skin

I'm STUCK!

Eats...
Yum!

Cute mushrooms sprout from
An underground fungus snarl
That feasts on dead things.

Witches' Butter

Bleeding
Milk
Cap

When you see a little mushroom on the forest
floor, you're only seeing the tip of an iceberg.
The biggest part of the fungus lurks underground
and sometimes reaches for miles, connecting
a network of other fungi and plants. One of
the largest living things on Earth is a fungus in
Oregon. It is estimated to be between 1,900 and
8,650 years old and sprawls underground for
almost 4 square miles (10 sq. km.).

MUSHROOMS

With names like lion's mane, inky caps, witches' butter, and bleeding milk cap, mushrooms can come in all sorts of shapes, colors, and sizes. Some are edible (even delicious!), some are medicinal, and some will flat-out kill you.

Mushrooms are neither plants nor animals. Along with mold, mildew, and yeast, mushrooms belong to their own kingdom of living things, which is called fungi. One of their biggest jobs is to eat and decompose dead stuff. Without them, we would be up to our armpits in dead plants and animals. So, thank you, fungi!

← Lion's Mane

Inky Caps
→

Each butterfly is
Oozy caterpillar soup
Metamorphosized.

chrysalis
ⓑ
↓

↑
ⓐ
caterpillar

When a caterpillar curls up and creates a cocoon around itself, it's bye-bye caterpillar and hello caterpillar smoothie. The caterpillar digests itself and becomes a soupy ooze of different building blocks needed for becoming a butterfly. Some cells survive being digested and serve as the base connector for the rest of the cells to form around. Cells that become eyes, toes, wings, and tongues line up and divide to form grown-up butterfly parts. When the process is complete, the butterfly emerges.

ⓒ

ⓓ

ⓔ

butterfly

No sloth lives alone.

Their slime-green fur is crawling

With hundreds of moths.

Sloths really know how to blend into their environment. Mainly because much of the environment can actually grow on them. Algae, fungi, and moss grow well in their damp fur, turning the sloth green and giving it a jungle aroma. The color and the scent protect the sloth from predators that hunt by sight and smell.

← sloth

Moths, beetles, and other insects are then drawn to the algae-covered animal. They feast on the algae and fungi, find mates in the fur, and lay their eggs in the sloth's poop. One sloth can be home to thousands of living things.

Sloths are portable ecosystems. Some species of birds hover and swoop over the sloths, picking off the delicious insects living on these slow-moving creatures.
When insects that live on a sloth die, the algae and fungi reabsorb their bodies and turn the insect remains into fertilizer, which keeps the algae growing. It takes a village!

Medical maggots,

Tiny surgeons on the scene,

Feasting on dead flesh.

Marvelous Medical Maggots

Hungry? So are maggots—and luckily for anyone with an infected open wound, maggots actually eat bacteria that can cause infections! This sounds disgusting, but it is in fact a really helpful thing. During the US Civil War (1860–1865), soldiers who were injured in battle often had piles of writhing maggots placed in their open wounds. The maggots gobbled up the bacteria and helped keep the wounds clean so they could heal. Maggot therapy is still sometimes used today to get rid of harmful bacteria in wounds. Bring on the creepy crawlies!

Holla!

Pink, eellike hagfish

Slide face-first into their lunch

Slurping up dead whale.

Long, tubular hagfish are some of the first responders to a death in the sea. They wriggle through the water like fat, fleshy ribbons and bury their heads in a corpse to feed from the inside out.

When a hagfish feels threatened, it sweats buckets of fibrous, mucousy slime. This makes it not only slippery but also dangerous. The slime immediately clogs up the gills and mouthparts of anything that tries to eat it.

Oh, and their jawless sucker mouths are lined with teeth and surrounded by hairy, wormy tentacles. So, enjoy that.

SLIME

EW!

Terrible teeth

Cute koala bear
Baby nuzzles Mama's butt,
Munches poop. Still cute?

Mama
koala
- - -

- - - - - - - Joey

- - - - - - - poop

When a baby koala, or joey, is hungry, Mama koala offers a soupy material, which is full of protein, called pap. But don't kid yourself. This "pap" is really poop ◆ and it comes right out of her butt. It may sound hideous, but the microorganisms in the pap are necessary for the baby to ingest so that, when it grows up, it will be able to break down tough, fiber-rich eucalyptus plants. Joeys feed on pap smoothies for a few weeks until they are ready to exit the pouch and dine on leaves.

EW!

SUPER GROSS

Blue
Whale
fart →

A car-sized bubble
Rises up from the deep sea
A giant whale fart!

CAR-SIZED
FART
BUBBLE

↑ car   fart ➡ - - - - - - - - - - - - - - - - - ←

All mammals create intestinal gases when they break down food. You know it. You live it.

Since whales are mammals, this happens to them too. Whales take enormous gulps of water filled with shrimplike krill, close their mouths, and push out the water with their school bus–sized tongues. Plates of thin, bonelike baleen hang from their jaws and act as filters trapping the krill—which they swallow, shell and all. Their digestive tracts have a lot of work to do to break down this meal. Big mammal, big meal, big gas. Do the math. A blue whale can make a fart bubble big enough for a horse to roam around in.

Is it raining? No!

That is a lobster peeing

Right out of its face.

Lobsters are crustaceans, which means they are soft-bodied animals inside a shell. Like all animals, they eat food and produce waste. The shell makes getting rid of that waste a challenge, so lobsters have a few work-arounds. They excrete waste through their gills and also through digestive glands in their abdomens. And they have a couple of nozzles right beneath their eyes, attached to bladder sacs, which allow them to pee right out of their faces!

Lobsters use face-peeing as a kind of love language. If you are a female lobster, you get a male's attention by peeing from your face into his home. Nice.

If you are a male lobster, one way to show how big and strong you are is by peeing into the face of your male rivals. This feat is very impressive to the females. Aren't you glad you aren't a lobster?

Lobster

←

WHAT IS HAIKU, ANYWAY?

Originally from Japan, a traditional haiku is a short, three-line poem with seventeen syllables. The first line has five syllables, the second has seven, and the third has five. Yet there's more to haiku than the number of syllables. These poems are a way of looking at the natural world, conveying deep wonder, and pondering the very nature of existence. A haiku is a provocative, brief breath of fresh air that leaves the reader stirred, changed, and enlightened. People have been writing haiku since the 1600s.

WHAT IS *HAIKU, EW*?

Just as traditional haiku focuses on glimpsing nature, juxtaposing images, and creating a sudden sense of clarity, so too does a *haiku, ew*. Because beyond its beauty, so much of nature is surprisingly gross. *Haiku, ew* celebrates the whole picture, letting the reader revel in the full splendor of the natural world. I hope these haiku surprise, revolt, and delight you!

WRITE YOUR OWN HAIKU

Pick a subject: an animal, a feeling, an idea, a moment in time, or something you saw. Have fun with this! Don't worry about the syllable counting at this stage. Just get your idea down on paper.

Describe the object or the moment. Think about what it looks like, what it smells or sounds like, what it feels like, and how it makes you feel. Make a list of words.

Then set up the haiku, shaping the thoughts into three lines with five, seven, and five syllables, respectively. Keep in mind that you are bringing the reader on a journey to see, feel, and hear what you are showing them.

TRY YOUR HAND AT *HAIKU, EW*!

Find something in nature that is remarkable, surprising, and kind of gross. Use that to set up a haiku that allows the reader to feel the moment with all their senses. Surprise and delight the reader by illuminating the mind-blowing wonder of nature along with a startling ick factor.

FIND OUT MORE ABOUT . . .

TOADS! Surinam toads are found throughout South America. Discover more about them from *National Geographic* (https://www.nationalgeographic.com/animals/amphibians/facts/surinam-toad). View a video of the actual birth process.

FLAMINGOS! Who doesn't love a tall pink bird that hangs out in huge groups with its friends and rests on one leg? Learn more about these beauties by visiting the San Diego Zoo online at https://animals.sandiegozoo.org/animals/flamingo.

FISH! You may think fish are quiet, but they're not! Fish hum, click, whistle, sizzle, burp, grunt, groan, jingle, and bark, among other sounds. You can hear them by visiting https://fishsounds.net/index.js.

BEES! There are at least twenty thousand different species of bees buzzing around the planet but only seven that actually make honey. Learn more about bees and even make a house to invite them into your yard (they won't sting!) with *Turn This Book into a Beehive!* by me, Lynn Brunelle.

GLOWWORMS! If you want to see a glowworm cave in real life, you have to go to New Zealand or Australia. But don't worry, you can see them online by visiting *National Geographic*: https://www.xrportal.io/animals/glow-worm-caves-of-new-zealand-national-geographic/.

FROGS! They start out in the water and end up on land. Learn more about their life cycle in *From Tadpole to Frog* by Wendy Pfeffer. There are over five thousand species of frogs on the planet. That's a lot of frogs! In *Fabulous Frogs* by Martin Jenkins, you can see a variety of them. *The Frog Book* by Steve Jenkins and Robin Page, is also fun. And if you are really hardcore about frogs, check out *The Book of Frogs: A Life-Size Guide to Six Hundred Species from around the World* by Tim Halliday.

MUSHROOMS! Fungi grow all over the world, favoring places that are shady and moist. Get to know them better in *The Mushroom Fan Club* by Elise Gravell.

BUTTERFLIES! There are nearly twenty thousand species of butterflies living all over the world (except Antarctica). Find out more about these colorful insects and the scientists who have studied them in *The Girl Who Drew Butterflies* by Joyce Sidman.

SLOTHS! Sloths are native to the tropical rainforests of Central and South America. Meet some of these adorable creatures from the Sloth Sanctuary of Costa Rica in *A Little Book of Sloth* and *Life in the Sloth Lane*, both by Lucy Cooke, and get an up-close look at the work of a sloth scientist in *The Adventures of Dr. Sloth* by Suzi Eszterhas.

MAGGOTS! Maggots are not the only surprising medical treatments humans have used. For more medical marvels, check out *Bat Spit, Maggots, and Other Amazing Medical Wonders* by Kristi Lew.

HAGFISH! Hagfish live on the bottom of the ocean floor and are the darlings of the slime world. Discover more about them and enjoy a revolting romp into the world of icky defense strategies in *Gross as a Snot Otter* by Jess Keating.

KOALAS! These non-bear beasties are native to Australia. Why do they eat dirt? How big are they when they are born? See for yourself at https://sdzwildlifeexplorers.org/animals/koala.

WHALES! There is so much to be dazzled by when it comes to whales. Did you know that some of them can weigh up to 400,000 pounds (181,437 kg)? Find out more in *The World of Whales: Get to Know the Giants of the Ocean* by Darcy Dobell and illustrated by Becky Thorns.

LOBSTERS! Did you know these ocean dwellers taste with their legs, chew with their stomachs, and have clear blood? They're wicked cool! Want to learn more? Check out the Lobster Institute from the University of Maine: https://umaine.edu/lobsterinstitute/educational-resources/lobsters/.